COPYCARD

A COPYCAT
DRAWING BOOK
by
Sally Kilroy

PUFFIN BOOKS

For Tom

HOW TO MAKE AND DRAW YOUR OWN CARDS

This book is full of ideas you can copy to make cards for lots of special occasions. Read the hints on these two pages before you start.

SPACING THINGS OUT

Get a piece of strong paper or card and fold it in half.
Then you can stand it up on the long or short side.

Now draw your picture on the front. Leave enough room for the whole picture or the clown might lose his shoes!

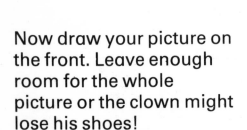

Happy
Birthday
SAM
love from
Alison
X

Write your greeting inside spaced out like this.

You could write it in pencil first to make sure it will fit.

There are letters and numbers to help you on the last page.

EXTRAS

You can stick glitter and stars and cotton wool on some cards.

You could give the three kings cotton wool or knitting wool whiskers and add glitter to their robes.

Draw a dark sky around the snowman and stick stars in it.

CUT-OUT CARDS

Some of the drawings would look lovely if you cut them out. Make a hole at the top and hang them up with a piece of bright wool or ribbon.

Write your greeting on the back.

BIRTHDAYS

A CLOWN

Draw a face with
a big red nose
and a white
mouth.

Then draw some
untidy hair and
add a little hat.

Add a top and
hands.

NUMBERS

Draw a large number and then decorate it.
Draw a scene or make a pattern inside the number.
Copy other numbers from the back of the book.

Now draw a pair
of very big
trousers.

Add silly shoes
and colour your
clown.

A BIRTHDAY CAKE

Draw the right
number of candles on
a big iced cake and
put it on a plate. You
can decorate the cake
with birds or the
person's name.

JACK-IN-THE-BOX

Fold your paper in half.

Colour the front blue and add some stars.

Inside the top half draw Jack springing up.

A LION

Draw a face with little ears and a frizzy mane.

Add a body and paws with big claws.
Then add a tail and sit him on a tub.

Add your message.

Draw one very big star on the bottom half and colour the sky dark blue.

Write your greeting inside the star.
What a surprise when it's opened!

Happy
Birthday
EMMA
Love from Tom

It is still nice to send a late card.

Draw an elephant because they never forget!

I am sorry, I forgot

CHRISTMAS

SANTA CLAUS

Draw a face with a beard.

Put him in a red suit and hood with furry edges.

Add a big belt and boots and give him a sack.

THE THREE KINGS

Draw three different kings each carrying a gift.

A CHRISTMAS TREE

Draw a tree in a tub with a bow.

Put an angel on top and decorate the tree.

Then add some presents.

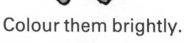

Colour them brightly.

THE CRIB SCENE

Draw a crib.

Put in a baby with a halo.

Now draw Mary

A CHRISTMAS STOCKING

If you draw a very large one you could cut it out.

Draw a stocking.

Then colour it.

Now fill it with toys.

and Joseph.

Put them all in a
stable with a big
star above it.

A SNOWMAN

Draw a snowman with a
hat and scarf.

Happy
Christmas

Don't forget your greeting!

EASTER

EASTER BUNNIES

Rabbits are often
seen on
Easter cards.

Draw a head with
very tall ears.

Add a body, arms
and big feet.

Draw a family of
bunnies.

CHICKS

Draw a fluffy chick.

Then draw another one hatching.

DECORATED EGGS

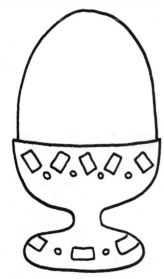 

Draw an egg in an egg-cup.

Then draw patterns or faces on the eggs.

Happy Easter from Caroline

Add your greeting.

PARTY INVITATIONS

You can write your invitations like this.

> Sam Brown
>
> invites: Lucy
>
> to a: BIRTHDAY PARTY
>
> on: Monday 3rd May
>
> from: 3.30 till 6.00 p.m.
>
> at: 7 Red Street
>
> Weymouth
>
> Please let me know if you can come.

PLACE NAMES

Show people where to sit by making little name cards.
Fold small pieces of paper like this. Then write each person's name on one.

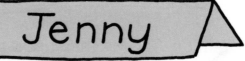

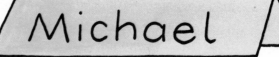

Here are some other ways to decorate your invitations.

A WOBBLY JELLY

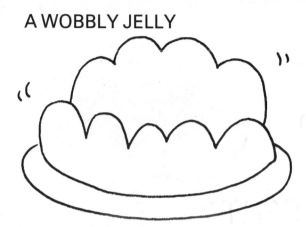 

Draw a big wobbly jelly on a plate.

Then add cherries, cream and hundreds and thousands.

A CRACKER

Draw a tube squeezed in near each end.

Draw a face in the middle.

Then decorate the cracker.

A PIRATE PARTY

Captain Ben
invites Jake to a
PIRATE PARTY
on Tuesday 7th June
from 3·00 - 6·00 p.m.
at 11 Mill Road

R.S.V.P.

A REPLY

Jake Thompson
thanks Captain Ben
for his invitation to a
PIRATE PARTY
on Tuesday 7th June
from 3·00 - 6·00 p.m.
at 11 Mill Road

He will be there.

A CLOWN PARTY   AN ANIMAL PARTY   A WILD WEST PARTY

A SPACE PARTY

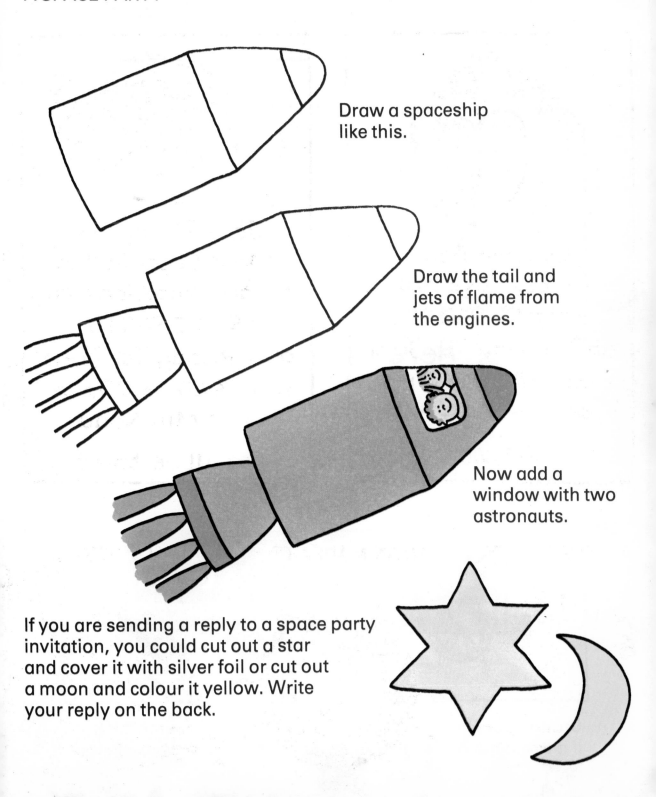

Draw a spaceship
like this.

Draw the tail and
jets of flame from
the engines.

Now add a
window with two
astronauts.

If you are sending a reply to a space party
invitation, you could cut out a star
and cover it with silver foil or cut out
a moon and colour it yellow. Write
your reply on the back.

THANK YOU LETTERS

You could write a letter like this to someone who has given you a present.

Dear Granny,

   Thank you for the lovely train. I like it very much.

   Here is a picture of it.

Love from

   James X

Draw the present you were given at the bottom of the letter. If it was a hat or a scarf you could draw yourself wearing it.

GOOD LUCK

Here are some things that are meant to bring good luck.

A LADYBIRD

Draw the body.   Add the spots,   then the head and legs.
                                                 Put the ladybird in
                                                 some grass.

A HORSESHOE

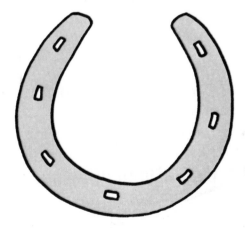

A FOUR-LEAFED
CLOVER

Draw a horseshoe with
slits for the nails to go
through.
This would look very nice if
you cut it out.

Draw a four-leafed clover
like this.
Don't forget to add your
message.

Camden. P. L

HALLOWE'EN

A WITCH ON A BROOMSTICK

Draw a face with a big hooked nose, a tall pointed hat and spiky hair.

Sit her on a broomstick.

Draw her feet. You can add a black cat.
Draw a big yellow moon behind them. Then you can cut out your drawing.

Draw the head and shoulders and two holes for the eyes.

Colour the eyes, draw the rest of the ghost floating along and then colour the background.

A CAULDRON

Have a
spooky
Hallowe'en

Add a creepy greeting.

Draw a big black pot on legs with a fire underneath. Add some bubbling brew to the pot and draw some bats flapping around.

MOTHER'S DAY

Draw a mother bear
wearing a pretty dress and
necklace.

Then draw a little bear next
to her.

A BASKET OF FLOWERS

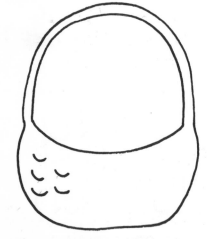

Draw a basket with a long
handle.

Fill it with flowers and tie a
bow on top.
Add little birds flying round it.

Write your greeting
inside the card.

Happy Mother's Day

FATHER'S DAY

Draw something that your father likes doing, such as fishing.

Draw your father's face, woolly sweater and hands.

Then add trousers, boots and a bag.

Now give him a rod with a big fish hanging from it.

A FAMILY OUTING

HAPPY FATHER'S DAY

Draw a car like this and put all the family in it.

GET WELL

Draw an unhappy face
with a sad bear next to it.

Add a pillow and a
headboard.

AN AMBULANCE

Draw a van with lights,
bumpers, wheels and a
door.

Then add the driver, a
flashing light and a sign on
the side.

Leave a space and draw the bottom of the bed.

Then add the sheet and blanket.

If you know what is the matter, you can draw that. Your friend might have measles – or a broken leg.

Add your message.

GET WELL SOON
love from Nicky X

A NEW BABY

Draw a smiling face with not much hair.

Then draw a playsuit with arms, legs and feet.

A BABY IN A PRAM

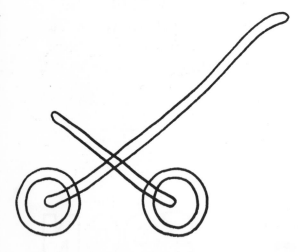

Draw an X with one long side and add wheels.

Then draw the rest of the pram with a hood and show the baby peeping out.

A RATTLE

Add little hands and colour it all.

Draw a rattle like this for the baby.

A DUCK
Draw a duck for the baby to play with.

Draw a head and an eye and a beak.

Write your message inside.

Draw the wing and the body with a stumpy tail.

Then draw webbed feet.

Hello, new baby

MOVING HOUSE

A MOVING VAN

Draw a van with a sign on the side. Put a ramp down.

A PACKING CASE

Draw a big box and put some labels on it.

Then draw some things sticking out of it. You can add some other things waiting to go in.

Add lots of things being loaded.

A HOUSE

Draw a house and colour it brightly.

I hope
you like
your
new house

Add your greeting.

HOLIDAYS

Send a card to people at home when you go away.
You can get blank postcards to draw on.

A SANDCASTLE

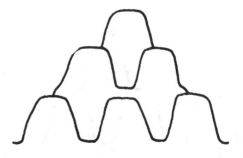

Start with three buckets of
sand.

Then build on top of them.

A PICNIC

Draw a face.

Add a body and
arms with one
hand holding a
sandwich.

Draw the rest of
the person sitting
cross-legged.

Put a flag on top of the castle and add some shells and a starfish.

Draw the sky and sea with some little boats in the background.

Draw another person and sit both on a rug with the rest of the picnic.

ALPHABET

A B C D E F G
H I J K L M N
O P Q R S T U
V W X Y Z

You can make up words like this.

HAPPY BIRTHDAY
POLLY

NUMBERS

Put them together to make bigger numbers.

1 2 3 4 5
6 7 8 9 0

14